Deliciously Easy Recipes
Prep Time of 15 minutes or less!

This edition is a revised and enlarged version of the **BEST RECIPES DELICIOUSLY EASY RECIPES** cookbook.

© **1992 Campbell Soup Company.**
"Campbell's" and "M'm! M'm! Good!" are registered trademarks of Campbell Soup Company.

This edition was produced by Campbell Soup Company's Publications Center, Campbell Soup Company, Campbell Place, Camden, NJ 08103-1799.

Corporate Editor: Pat Teberg
Assistant Editor: Alice Joy Carter
Creative Director: Stacy-Jo Mannella
Campbell Kitchens: Nancy DeBenedetta
Marketing Manager: Eugene Sung
Public Relations Manager: Kevin Lowery
Photography: Sacco Productions Limited/Chicago
Photographers: Catherine Money, Laurie Proffitt
Photo Stylists/Production: Betty Karslake, Paula Walters
Food Stylists: Donna Coates, Carol Parik
Assistant Food Stylist: Moisette Sintov McNerney

This edition published by:
Publications International, Ltd.
7373 N. Cicero Avenue
Lincolnwood, Illinois 60646

ISBN: 1-56173-891-3

Pictured on the front cover: Lemon-Broccoli Chicken (*recipe page 16*).

Pictured on the back cover, clockwise from top right: Chicken Broccoli Orientale over Broth-Simmered Rice (*recipes page 28*), Simple Salisbury Steak (*recipe page 58*) and Broccoli Bake (*recipe page 86*).

Manufactured in U.S.A.

8 7 6 5 4 3 2 1

Preparation and Cooking Times: Each of these recipes was developed and tested in Campbell Kitchens by professional home economists. The preparation times are based on the approximate amount of time required to assemble the recipe *before* baking, cooking, chilling, freezing or serving. These times include preparation steps such as chopping; mixing; cooking rice, pasta, vegetables; etc. The fact that some preparations can be done simultaneously is taken into account. The standing times referred to just before serving are not included in these cooking times.

Microwave Cooking Times: Microwave cooking times in this book are approximate. These recipes have been tested in 650- to 700-watt microwave ovens. Foods cooked in lower-wattage ovens may require longer cooking times. Use the cooking times as guidelines and check for doneness before adding more time.

Great Cooking Begins with Campbell's Soups

G reat things happen when you begin with Campbell's Soups. The delicious flavor packed inside every can or package of Campbell's Soup eliminates the need for a lot of extra ingredients *and* helps you streamline preparation steps. Choose from Campbell's traditional favorite soups, such as Tomato, Cream of Mushroom, Cream of Celery and Cream of Chicken, or the newer varieties—Cream of Broccoli and Broccoli Cheese—and you'll have the beginnings of many *quick, easy* and *delicious* recipes.

All the great-tasting dishes in *Deliciously Easy Recipes* were created by a team of experienced home economists in the Campbell Kitchens. Every recipe in this cookbook has its own mouth-watering photograph so you'll know what it looks like even before you begin cooking. And, as you turn these pages, you'll find lots of timesaving kitchen tips, handy ingredient substitutions and easy serving suggestions.

Whether you're looking for recipes to serve any day of the week or recipes especially for company, you'll find them here in *Deliciously Easy Recipes*. From our Kitchens to yours, we give you these Campbell favorites—they're M'm! M'm! Good!

Campbell's Family of Cooking Soups

M'm! M'm! Good!®
Snacks & Soups

Nachos

This creamy mixture of cheese soup and salsa will remind you of Mexican-style Chili con Queso. Depending upon how spicy you want it, use either hot, medium or mild salsa to make the sauce.

> **1 can (11 ounces) Campbell's condensed Cheddar cheese soup**
> **½ cup salsa**
> **1 bag (about 10 ounces) tortilla chips for dipping**
> **Chopped tomato, sliced green onions, sliced pitted ripe olives *and/or* chopped green or sweet red pepper**

1. In 1½-quart saucepan, combine soup and salsa. Over medium heat, heat until hot and bubbling, stirring occasionally.

2. Arrange tortilla chips evenly on serving platter. Spoon sauce over chips. Top with tomato, onions, olives and/or chopped pepper.

Makes about 1½ cups sauce or 6 appetizer servings	Prep Time: 10 minutes Cook Time: 5 minutes

To microwave: In 1½-quart microwave-safe casserole, combine soup and salsa. Microwave, uncovered, on HIGH 2½ minutes or until hot and bubbling, stirring halfway through cooking. Serve as directed in step 2.

Broccoli-Cheese Dip

1 can (10¾ ounces) Campbell's condensed broccoli cheese soup
1 package (10 ounces) frozen chopped broccoli, thawed and
　　drained
1 medium tomato, chopped
½ cup sour cream
2 teaspoons Dijon-style mustard
　　Assorted crackers *and* chips for dipping

1. In medium bowl, combine soup, broccoli, tomato, sour cream and
   mustard. Cover; refrigerate at least 4 hours before serving.

2. Serve with crackers and chips for dipping.

Makes about 3 cups or 12 appetizer servings	Prep Time: 5 minutes Chill Time: 4 hours

Tip: To quickly thaw a package of frozen chopped broccoli, use your microwave oven. Place frozen broccoli in a 1½-quart microwave-safe casserole. Cover with lid; microwave on HIGH 1 to 2 minutes or until broccoli can be easily separated. Drain the broccoli in a sieve and then you are ready to make this dip.

Tip: Bread sticks, pita bread chips, bagel chips or pretzels can also be used as dippers for this dip.

Tomato French Onion Soup

1 can (10¾ ounces) Campbell's condensed tomato soup
1 can (10½ ounces) Campbell's condensed French onion soup
2 soup cans water
   Toasted bread quarters *or* croutons
   Grated Parmesan cheese
   Fresh thyme sprigs for garnish

1. In 2-quart saucepan, combine tomato soup and onion soup. Add water. Over medium heat, heat through, stirring occasionally.

2. Top each bowl of soup with bread and cheese. Garnish with thyme, if desired.

Makes about 5 cups or 5 side-dish servings	Prep Time: 5 minutes Cook Time: 10 minutes

Tomato Beef Stew

Serve this easy, hearty stew with cheese-topped garlic bread, if you like.

½ pound ground beef
1 can (10¾ ounces) Campbell's condensed tomato soup
½ soup can water
1 cup frozen cut green beans
½ cup frozen sliced carrots
1 teaspoon Worcestershire sauce

1. In 1½-quart saucepan over medium heat, cook beef until browned and no longer pink, stirring to separate meat. Spoon off fat.

2. Stir in soup and water. Add beans, carrots and Worcestershire sauce. Heat to simmering. Cook 10 minutes or until vegetables are tender, stirring occasionally.

Makes about 3 cups or 2 main-dish servings	Prep Time: 5 minutes Cook Time: 20 minutes

Tomato French Onion Soup (top) *and*
Tomato Beef Stew (bottom)

Mac 'n' Tomato Soup

Accompany this spicy chili-flavored soup with warm flour tortillas or corn bread, if you like.

   ¼ pound ground beef
   1 can (10¾ ounces) Campbell's condensed tomato soup
   1 soup can water
   ¼ cup *dry* corkscrew *or* elbow macaroni
   2 teaspoons chili powder

1. In 1½-quart saucepan over medium heat, cook beef until browned and no longer pink, stirring to separate meat. Spoon off fat.

2. Stir in soup and water. Add macaroni and chili powder. Heat to simmering. Cook 15 minutes or until macaroni is tender, stirring occasionally.

Makes about 2½ cups or 2 side-dish servings	Prep Time: 5 minutes Cook Time: 25 minutes

Taco Soup

To add zip to this Mexican-style soup, substitute shredded Monterey Jack cheese with jalapeño peppers for the Cheddar cheese.

   1 can (10¾ ounces) Campbell's condensed tomato soup
   1 soup can water
   ¼ cup salsa
   Crumbled tortilla chips
   Shredded Cheddar *or* Monterey Jack cheese
   Sliced green onion
   Sour cream

1. In 1½-quart saucepan, combine soup, water and salsa. Over medium heat, heat through, stirring occasionally.

2. Sprinkle *each* serving with tortilla chips, cheese and onion; top with a spoonful of sour cream.

Makes about 2½ cups or 2 side-dish servings	Prep Time: 5 minutes Cook Time: 5 minutes

Mac 'n' Tomato Soup (top) *and*
Taco Soup (bottom)

Shrimp Creole Soup

    1 can (10¾ ounces) Campbell's condensed tomato soup
    1 soup can water
    ½ green pepper, chopped
    ½ small onion, chopped
    ½ cup cooked rice
    ½ cup coarsely chopped cooked shrimp
    ¼ teaspoon Louisiana-style hot sauce
        Fresh dill sprigs for garnish

In 1½-quart saucepan, combine soup and water. Add pepper, onion, rice, shrimp and hot sauce. Over medium heat, heat through, stirring occasionally. Garnish with dill, if desired.

Makes about 3½ cups or 3 side-dish servings	Prep Time: 10 minutes Cook Time: 5 minutes

Vegetable Beef Soup

Create your own combination of vegetables to make this savory soup. You'll need a total of 4 cups of frozen mixed vegetables.

    2 cans (10½ ounces *each*) Campbell's condensed beef broth
    1 soup can water
    2 medium potatoes, cubed
    1 package (16 ounces) frozen mixed vegetables
    1 can (about 8 ounces) tomatoes, undrained and cut up
    1 cup cubed cooked beef
    ¼ teaspoon dried thyme leaves, crushed
    ⅛ teaspoon pepper

In 3-quart saucepan, combine broth, water and potatoes. Over high heat, heat to boiling. Reduce heat to low. Cover; cook 5 minutes or until potatoes are tender. Add remaining ingredients. Cover; heat to simmering. Cook until vegetables are tender.

Makes about 7½ cups or 6 side-dish servings	Prep Time: 10 minutes Cook Time: 20 minutes

Shrimp Creole Soup (top) *and*
Vegetable Beef Soup (bottom)

Tomato-Vegetable Noodle Soup

A medley of zucchini strips, corn, sliced carrot and sliced mushrooms was used to make this soup.

    1 can (10¾ ounces) Campbell's condensed tomato soup
    1 soup can water
    1 cup cooked mixed vegetables
    1 cup cooked bow tie noodles (1 cup dry)

In 1½-quart saucepan, combine soup and water. Add vegetables and noodles. Over medium heat, heat through, stirring occasionally.

Makes about 3½ cups or 3 side-dish servings	Prep Time: 5 minutes Cook Time: 5 minutes

Chicken Noodle Soup

    2 cans (10½ ounces *each*) Campbell's condensed chicken broth
    2 soup cans water
    ¼ cup chopped celery
    ¼ cup chopped carrot
    1 tablespoon finely chopped onion
    1 tablespoon chopped fresh parsley
    ⅛ teaspoon poultry seasoning
    ⅛ teaspoon dried thyme leaves, crushed
    2 cups diced cooked chicken *or* turkey
    1 cup cooked medium egg noodles (1 cup dry)

1. In 3-quart saucepan, combine broth, water, celery, carrot, onion, parsley, poultry seasoning and thyme. Over medium heat, heat to boiling, stirring occasionally.

2. Reduce heat to low. Cover; cook 20 minutes or until vegetables are tender, stirring occasionally. Add chicken and noodles; heat through.

Makes about 7 cups or 4 main-dish servings	Prep Time: 15 minutes Cook Time: 30 minutes

**Tomato-Vegetable Noodle Soup (top) *and*
Chicken Noodle Soup (bottom)**

M'm! M'm! Good!
Poultry

Lemon-Broccoli Chicken

This delicious six-ingredient entrée was specially developed using Campbell's cream of broccoli soup. Also pictured on the front cover.

1 lemon
1 tablespoon vegetable oil
4 skinless, boneless chicken breast halves (about 1 pound)
1 can (10¾ ounces) Campbell's condensed cream of broccoli soup
¼ cup milk
⅛ teaspoon pepper
Fresh marjoram sprigs *and* carrot curls for garnish

1. Cut 4 thin slices from lemon; set aside. Squeeze 2 *teaspoons* juice from remaining lemon; set aside.

2. In 10-inch skillet over medium-high heat, in hot oil, cook chicken 10 minutes or until browned on both sides. Spoon off fat.

3. In bowl, combine soup and milk. Stir in reserved lemon juice and pepper; pour over chicken. Top chicken with lemon slices.

4. Reduce heat to low. Cover; cook 5 minutes or until chicken is no longer pink, stirring occasionally. Garnish with marjoram and carrot curls, if desired.

Makes 4 main-dish servings	Prep Time: 5 minutes Cook Time: 15 minutes

Lemon-Broccoli Turkey: Prepare Lemon-Broccoli Chicken as directed above, *except* substitute 4 *raw turkey cutlets* (about 1 pound) for the chicken. In step 2, cook turkey about 8 minutes until turkey is browned and no longer pink. Continue as directed in step 3.

Chicken Broccoli Divan

Chicken Divan is one of Campbell's most requested recipes. This updated version is made with one of our newest condensed soups—broccoli cheese soup.

   1 pound broccoli, cut into 2-inch flowerets, cooked and drained
1½ cups cubed cooked chicken *or* turkey
   1 can (10¾ ounces) Campbell's condensed broccoli cheese soup
   ⅓ cup milk
   2 tablespoons dry bread crumbs
   1 tablespoon margarine *or* butter, melted

1. Preheat oven to 450°F. In 9-inch pie plate or 1½-quart casserole, arrange broccoli and chicken. In small bowl, combine soup and milk. Pour over broccoli and chicken.

2. In cup, combine bread crumbs and margarine; sprinkle over top. Bake 10 minutes or until hot.

Makes 4 main-dish servings	Prep Time: 10 minutes Cook Time: 10 minutes

To microwave: In 9-inch microwave-safe pie plate, arrange broccoli and chicken. In small bowl, combine soup and milk. Pour over broccoli and chicken. In cup, combine bread crumbs and margarine; sprinkle over top. Cover with waxed paper; microwave on HIGH 6 minutes or until hot, rotating dish halfway through heating.

Tip: To vary the flavor of this 20-minute casserole, sprinkle ½ cup shredded *Cheddar cheese* or 2 tablespoons grated *Parmesan cheese* over soup mixture *before* topping with the crumb mixture.

Chicken Broccoli Divan

Garden Chicken and Stuffing

If you don't have already-cooked chicken in the refrigerator, use cooked chicken purchased from the supermarket deli to make this recipe.

¼ cup margarine *or* butter
1 cup chopped celery
1 cup chopped onion
1 cup chopped carrots
¼ cup all-purpose flour
1 can (10½ ounces) Campbell's condensed chicken broth
1 cup milk
1 package (7 ounces) herb seasoned cubed stuffing
2 cups cubed cooked chicken *or* turkey
1 cup shredded Cheddar cheese (4 ounces)
   Celery leaves *and* carrot curl for garnish

1. In 3-quart saucepan over medium heat, in hot margarine, cook celery, onion and carrots until tender. Add flour; cook 1 minute more, stirring constantly. Gradually stir in broth and milk. Cook until mixture boils and thickens, stirring constantly.

2. Add stuffing and chicken; toss to coat. Spoon into 2-quart oblong baking dish. Bake at 350°F. for 35 minutes. Sprinkle with cheese. Bake 5 minutes more or until cheese melts. Garnish with celery leaves and carrot curl, if desired.

Makes 6 main-dish servings	Prep Time: 15 minutes Cook Time: 40 minutes

Glorified Chicken Bake

A popular Campbell recipe since 1957, this three-ingredient main dish can be cooked in the oven or on top of the range.

2½- to 3-pound broiler-fryer chicken, cut up
 1 tablespoon margarine *or* butter, melted
 1 can (10¾ ounces) Campbell's condensed cream of chicken soup
 Fresh rosemary sprigs *and* green and sweet red pepper strips
 for garnish

1. In 2-quart oblong baking dish, arrange chicken skin-side up. Drizzle with margarine. Bake at 375°F. for 40 minutes.

2. Spoon soup over chicken. Bake 20 minutes more or until chicken is no longer pink and juices run clear.

3. To serve, arrange chicken on serving platter. Stir sauce and spoon over chicken. Garnish with rosemary and pepper strips, if desired.

Makes 4 main-dish servings	Prep Time: 5 minutes Cook Time: 60 minutes

Glorified Chicken Skillet: Use same ingredients as above in Glorified Chicken Bake, *except* omit the margarine. In 10-inch skillet over medium-high heat, heat 2 tablespoons *vegetable oil* until hot. Cook chicken 10 minutes or until browned on all sides. Spoon off fat. Stir in soup. Reduce heat to low. Cover; cook 35 minutes or until chicken is no longer pink and juices run clear, stirring occasionally. Serve as directed in step 3.

Tip: Substitute 4 chicken legs (about 2 pounds) for the broiler-fryer chicken.

Souper Choices: Substitute any one of the following soups for the cream of chicken soup: 1 can (10¾ ounces) Campbell's condensed *cream of broccoli soup, cream of celery soup* or *cream of mushroom soup.*

Glorified Chicken Bake

Easy Onion Chicken

Pictured here, Easy Onion Chicken is served with prepared long-grain and wild rice mix and sliced cucumbers and lettuce drizzled with clear Italian salad dressing.

1 pouch Campbell's dry onion quality soup and recipe mix
¾ cup dry bread crumbs
1 tablespoon grated Parmesan cheese
⅛ teaspoon pepper
6 skinless, boneless chicken breast halves *or* 12 skinless, boneless chicken thighs (about 1½ pounds)
2 eggs, beaten
2 tablespoons margarine *or* butter, melted
Thin strips green onion for garnish

1. With rolling pin, crush onion soup mix in pouch. On waxed paper, combine soup mix, bread crumbs, cheese and pepper.

2. Dip chicken in eggs; coat with crumb mixture.

3. On baking sheet, arrange chicken. Drizzle with margarine. Bake at 400°F. for 20 minutes or until chicken is no longer pink. Garnish with green onion, if desired.

Makes 6 main-dish servings	Prep Time: 10 minutes Cook Time: 20 minutes

The U.S. Department of Agriculture operates a toll-free Meat and Poultry Hotline to answer your food safety questions about meat and poultry. From 10 a.m. to 4 p.m. Eastern Standard Time, Monday through Friday, home economists will answer your meat and poultry questions—just dial 1-800-535-4555. If you are in the Washington, DC metropolitan area, dial (202) 447-3333.*

*Source: U.S. Department of Agriculture–Food Safety and Inspection Service.

Easy Onion Chicken

Everyday Broccoli Cheese Chicken

You can substitute 12 fresh asparagus spears, cut into 2-inch pieces, for the broccoli in this skillet entrée.

1 tablespoon margarine *or* butter
4 skinless, boneless chicken breast halves (about 1 pound)
1 can (10¾ ounces) Campbell's condensed broccoli cheese soup
⅓ cup water *or* milk
2 cups broccoli cut in 1½-inch pieces
⅛ teaspoon pepper
    Fresh sage leaves *and* cherry tomatoes for garnish

1. In 10-inch skillet over medium-high heat, in hot margarine, cook chicken 10 minutes or until browned on both sides. Spoon off fat.

2. Stir in soup and water. Add broccoli and pepper. Heat to boiling. Reduce heat to low. Cover; cook 10 minutes or until broccoli is tender and chicken is no longer pink, stirring occasionally. Garnish with sage and cherry tomatoes, if desired.

Makes 4 main-dish servings	Prep Time: 5 minutes Cook Time: 25 minutes

The safest way to thaw frozen poultry or meat is to defrost it in the refrigerator. Allow at least 24 hours for every 5 pounds of frozen poultry or meat. Never thaw frozen poultry or meat at room temperature. Try this quick method: Put the package of frozen poultry or meat in a watertight plastic bag and submerge the bag in cold water. Change the water every 30 minutes until poultry or meat is thawed. It will take 30 minutes to 1 hour to thaw 1 pound of frozen poultry or meat.*

*Source: U.S. Department of Agriculture-Food Safety and Inspection Service.

Chicken Broccoli Orientale

This saucy chicken main dish is served over Broth-Simmered Rice—a savory rice that also makes an ideal accompaniment for other entrées, too! Also pictured on the back cover.

   Broth-Simmered Rice (recipe follows) *or* hot cooked rice
1 tablespoon vegetable oil
1 pound skinless, boneless chicken breasts *or* thighs, cut into strips
1 small onion, cut into 1-inch pieces
1 medium sweet red *or* green pepper, cut into 1-inch squares
1 can (10¾ ounces) Campbell's condensed cream of broccoli soup
3 tablespoons water
1 tablespoon soy sauce
   Green onion for garnish
   Soy sauce

1. Prepare Broth-Simmered Rice as directed. Meanwhile, in 10-inch skillet over medium-high heat, in hot oil, cook *half* of chicken until browned. Remove; set aside. Repeat with remaining chicken.

2. Return chicken to skillet. Add onion and pepper. Cook 5 minutes or until vegetables are tender-crisp and chicken is no longer pink.

3. Stir in soup, water and 1 tablespoon soy sauce. Heat to boiling. Reduce heat to low. Cover; cook 5 minutes, stirring occasionally.

4. Serve chicken mixture over rice. Garnish with green onion and pass additional soy sauce, if desired.

Makes about 3½ cups or 4 main-dish servings	Prep Time: 10 minutes Cook Time: 20 minutes

Broth-Simmered Rice: In 2-quart saucepan over medium-high heat, heat 1 can (10½ ounces) Campbell's condensed *chicken broth* and 1 soup can *water* to boiling. Stir in 1 cup uncooked *regular long-grain rice*. Reduce heat to low. Cover; cook 20 minutes or until rice is tender and liquid is absorbed. Makes about 3 cups.

Chicken Broccoli Orientale over
Broth-Simmered Rice

Skillet Chicken 'n' Noodles

1 tablespoon vegetable oil
4 skinless, boneless chicken breast halves (about 1 pound)
1 small onion, sliced
1 can (10½ ounces) Campbell's condensed chicken broth
2 cups *dry* medium egg noodles
½ cup water
½ teaspoon dried basil leaves, crushed
⅛ teaspoon pepper
1 package (16 ounces) desired frozen vegetable combination, thawed
1 tablespoon grated Parmesan cheese
    Very thin strips sweet red pepper for garnish

1. In 10-inch skillet over medium-high heat, in hot oil, cook chicken and onion 10 minutes or until chicken is browned on both sides. Remove; set aside. Spoon off fat.

2. In same skillet, combine broth, noodles, water, basil and pepper. Heat to boiling. Arrange chicken on top of noodles; top with vegetables. Cover; cook 10 minutes or until noodles and vegetables are done and chicken is no longer pink, stirring occasionally to keep noodles from sticking together.

3. Remove chicken. Transfer noodles and vegetable mixture to serving platter. Arrange chicken on top. Sprinkle with cheese. Garnish with red pepper, if desired.

Makes 4 main-dish servings	Prep Time: 5 minutes Cook Time: 25 minutes

Tip: You can create your own vegetable combination using a mixture of fresh and/or frozen vegetables. For example, combine 1 cup green beans cut in 1½-inch pieces, 1 cup carrot sticks, ½ cup broccoli flowerets and ½ cup diced sweet red pepper.

Savory Chicken-Stuffing Bake

1 package (6 ounces) instant chicken-flavored stuffing mix
6 skinless, boneless chicken breast halves (about 1½ pounds)
1 can (10¾ ounces) Campbell's condensed cream of chicken soup
⅓ cup milk
1 teaspoon chopped fresh *or* dried parsley
Paprika *and* watercress sprigs for garnish

1. Preheat oven to 400°F. Prepare stuffing mix according to package directions, but *do not let stand* as directed on package.

2. In 2-quart oblong baking dish, spoon stuffing down center of dish, leaving space on both sides of stuffing to arrange chicken. Arrange 3 chicken pieces on each side of stuffing, overlapping, if necessary.

3. In small bowl, combine soup and milk. Stir in parsley. Pour over chicken. Cover with foil; bake 15 minutes. Uncover; bake 10 minutes more or until chicken is no longer pink.

4. To serve, stir sauce at edges and spoon over chicken. Sprinkle with paprika. Garnish with watercress, if desired.

Makes 6 main-dish servings	Prep Time: 10 minutes Cook Time: 25 minutes

Souper Choice: Substitute 1 can (10¾ ounces) Campbell's condensed *cream of mushroom soup* for the cream of chicken soup.

When you buy chicken, look for a "sell by" label on the package. Most chicken processors specify the last day poultry should be sold. Avoid packages with expired dates.

Peach-Glazed Chicken

1 can (about 16 ounces) peaches in heavy syrup, undrained
1 pouch Campbell's dry onion quality soup and recipe mix
1 tablespoon brown sugar
1 teaspoon lemon juice
2 tablespoons margarine *or* butter
6 skinless, boneless chicken breast halves *or* 12 skinless, boneless chicken thighs (about 1½ pounds)
  Hot cooked parsley rice *or* Broth-Simmered Rice (see recipe, page 28)
  Sliced almonds, sliced fresh peaches *and* fresh savory leaves for garnish

1. In covered blender or food processor, combine peaches, soup mix, brown sugar and lemon juice. Blend until smooth; set aside.

2. Meanwhile, in 10-inch skillet over medium-high heat, in hot margarine, cook *half* of chicken 10 minutes or until browned on both sides. Remove; set aside. Repeat with remaining chicken. Spoon off fat.

3. Stir in peach mixture. Return chicken to skillet. Heat to boiling. Reduce heat to medium. Cook 10 minutes or until chicken is no longer pink, stirring occasionally.

4. Serve chicken and peach sauce with rice. Sprinkle with almonds and garnish with sliced peaches and savory, if desired.

Makes 6 main-dish servings	Prep Time: 5 minutes Cook Time: 35 minutes

It's best to cook chicken as soon as possible once you remove it from the refrigerator. Be sure to wash your hands, work surface, knives and utensils with hot, soapy water after you work with the chicken to prevent spreading bacteria to other foods.

Chicken-and-Cheese Fettuccine

Pictured here, saucy Chicken-and-Cheese Fettuccine is prepared with grilled chicken breasts. Pass additional grated Parmesan cheese and serve with a Caesar salad, if you like.

> **1 tablespoon margarine** *or* **butter**
> **1 clove garlic, minced**
> **1½ cups cooked chicken cut in strips**
> **1 can (10¾ ounces) Campbell's condensed broccoli cheese soup**
> **1 cup milk**
> **¼ cup grated Parmesan cheese**
> **3 cups hot cooked fettuccine (about 8 ounces dry)**
> **Chopped fresh parsley** *and* **kale leaves for garnish**

1. In 10-inch skillet over medium heat, in hot margarine, cook garlic 2 minutes, stirring constantly.

2. Stir in chicken, soup, milk and cheese. Heat to boiling. Reduce heat to low. Cook 5 minutes, stirring occasionally.

3. To serve, pour over fettuccine; toss to coat. Sprinkle with parsley and garnish with kale, if desired.

Makes about 5 cups or 4 main-dish servings	Prep Time: 10 minutes Cook Time: 15 minutes

Ham-and-Cheese Fettuccine: Prepare Chicken-and-Cheese Fettuccine as directed above, *except* substitute 1½ cups cooked *ham* cut in strips, (about 8 ounces) for the chicken.

Tip: To make 1½ cups cooked chicken strips, cook about ¾ pound boneless, skinless chicken breasts.

Chicken Broccoli Rice Skillet

The rice "cooks" in the broccoli-flavored sauce for this easy one-dish meal.

> **2 tablespoons margarine *or* butter**
> **1 pound skinless, boneless chicken breasts, cut into thin strips**
> **2 cups frozen broccoli cuts**
> **¾ cup sliced carrots**
> **1 can (10¾ ounces) Campbell's condensed cream of broccoli soup**
> **1 cup milk**
> **⅛ teaspoon pepper**
> **1¼ cups *uncooked* quick-cooking rice**

1. In 10-inch skillet over medium-high heat, in hot margarine, cook *half* of chicken until browned. Remove; set aside. Repeat with remaining chicken.

2. Add broccoli and carrots. Cook until tender-crisp, stirring occasionally.

3. Stir in soup, milk and pepper. Return chicken to skillet. Heat to boiling. Reduce heat to low. Cover; cook 10 minutes or until chicken is no longer pink, stirring occasionally.

4. Stir in rice. Cover; remove from heat. Let stand 5 minutes. Fluff mixture with fork before serving.

Makes about 5½ cups or 4 main-dish servings	**Prep Time: 10 minutes** **Cook Time: 30 minutes**

Use a sturdy plastic cutting board when cutting raw poultry or meat instead of a wooden board. Since wooden boards are porous, it is difficult to thoroughly wash them.

Ginger Chicken Stir-Fry

Broccoli, green onion, celery and carrots are used to make Ginger Chicken Stir-Fry. As pictured here, it is served on a bed of cellophane noodles (see Tip below).

> 3 tablespoons vegetable oil, divided
> 1 pound skinless, boneless chicken breasts *or* thighs, cut into strips
> 4 cups cut-up desired fresh vegetables
> 1 clove garlic, minced
> 1 can (10½ ounces) Campbell's condensed chicken broth
> 2 tablespoons cornstarch
> 1 tablespoon soy sauce
> ½ teaspoon ground ginger
>   Hot cooked noodles *or* rice
>   Toasted sliced almonds

1. In 10-inch skillet or wok over medium-high heat, in *2 tablespoons* hot oil, stir-fry *half* of chicken until browned and no longer pink. Remove; set aside. Repeat with remaining chicken.

2. In same skillet in remaining 1 tablespoon oil, stir-fry vegetables and garlic until tender-crisp.

3. Meanwhile, in small bowl, stir together cornstarch, soy sauce and ginger until smooth. Add to skillet along with reserved chicken. Cook until mixture boils and thickens, stirring constantly. Serve over noodles. Sprinkle with almonds.

Makes about 6 cups or 4 main-dish servings	Prep Time: 10 minutes Cook Time: 10 minutes

Tip: Cellophane noodles are available in the specialty sections of most supermarkets. The *dry* noodles can either be cooked in boiling water, drained and used as traditional noodles, or, as in the photograph, cooked briefly in hot oil until crispy.

Ginger Chicken Stir-Fry

Saucy Chicken and Noodles

Pictured here, Saucy Chicken and Noodles is served with buttered sliced carrots and garnished with fresh purple basil.

4 skinless, boneless chicken breast halves (about 1 pound)
1 can (10¾ ounces) Campbell's condensed broccoli cheese soup
⅓ cup milk
3 cups hot cooked medium egg noodles (3 cups dry)
Chopped fresh parsley for garnish

1. In 9-inch pie plate, arrange chicken. In small bowl, combine soup and milk. Pour over chicken.

2. Bake at 400°F. for 25 minutes or until chicken is no longer pink. Stir sauce before serving. Serve sauce over chicken and noodles. Garnish with parsley, if desired.

Makes 4 main-dish servings	Prep Time: 5 minutes Cook Time: 25 minutes

To microwave: In 9-inch microwave-safe pie plate, arrange chicken. In small bowl, combine soup and milk. Pour over chicken. Cover with waxed paper; microwave on HIGH 10 minutes or until chicken is no longer pink, rearranging chicken halfway through cooking. Let stand, covered, 5 minutes. Stir sauce before serving. Serve sauce over chicken and noodles. Garnish as directed in step 2.

Herbed Chicken Fricassee

Pictured here, Herbed Chicken Fricassee is served with tomato wedges and zucchini strips and garnished with fresh basil.

  2 tablespoons all-purpose flour
½ teaspoon Italian seasoning, crushed
⅛ teaspoon pepper
4 skinless, boneless chicken breast halves *or* **8 skinless, boneless chicken thighs (about 1 pound)**
2 tablespoons margarine *or* **butter**
1 can (10¾ ounces) Campbell's condensed cream of broccoli soup
1 can (about 16 ounces) stewed tomatoes, undrained
Hot cooked noodles *or* **rice**

1. On waxed paper, combine flour, Italian seasoning and pepper. Coat chicken lightly with flour mixture.

2. In 10-inch skillet over medium-high heat, in hot margarine, cook chicken 10 minutes or until chicken is browned on both sides and no longer pink. Push chicken to one side of skillet. Spoon off fat.

3. Add soup and tomatoes, stirring to loosen browned bits. Heat to boiling. Reduce heat to low. Cover; cook 5 minutes or until hot and bubbling.

4. To serve, arrange chicken over noodles. Spoon sauce over chicken.

Makes 4 main-dish servings	Prep Time: 5 minutes Cook Time: 20 minutes

Herbed Chicken Fricassee

Onion Chicken Stir-Fry

When you stir-fry, you cook foods fast! There just isn't time to stop cooking to cut up each vegetable. That's why you should cut and measure all of the ingredients before cooking. And don't forget the chopsticks!

   1 pouch Campbell's dry onion quality soup and recipe mix
   2 teaspoons cornstarch
  ¼ teaspoon ground ginger
   1 cup water
   1 tablespoon vegetable oil
   1 pound skinless, boneless chicken breasts *or* thighs, cut into strips
1½ cups broccoli flowerets
1½ cups sliced fresh mushrooms
   2 medium carrots, cut into matchstick-thin strips
     Hot cooked rice *or* Broth-Simmered Rice (see recipe, page 28)
     Fresh cilantro *or* parsley for garnish

1. In small bowl, combine soup mix, cornstarch, ginger and water; set aside.

2. In 10-inch skillet or wok over medium-high heat, in hot oil, stir-fry *half* of chicken until chicken is browned and no longer pink. Remove; set aside. Repeat with remaining chicken. Spoon off fat.

3. Return chicken to skillet. Stir in soup mixture. Heat to boiling, stirring constantly.

4. Add broccoli, mushrooms and carrots. Reduce heat to low. Cover; cook 5 minutes, stirring occasionally. Serve with rice. Garnish with cilantro, if desired.

Makes about 6 cups or 4 main-dish servings	Prep Time: 10 minutes Cook Time: 15 minutes

When shopping for skinless, boneless chicken breasts, the chicken meat should be light in color, not gray or pasty looking.

Ham-and-Cheese Chicken Rolls

Pictured here, a single serving of Ham-and-Cheese Chicken Rolls is served with a mixed garden vegetable salad and dark whole-grain bread.

 4 **skinless, boneless chicken breast halves (about 1 pound)**
 4 **thin slices (½ ounce *each*) cooked ham**
 4 **thin slices (½ ounce *each*) Swiss cheese**
 2 **tablespoons vegetable oil**
 1 **can (10¾ ounces) Campbell's condensed cream of broccoli soup**
 ⅓ **cup milk**
 ¼ **cup sliced green onions**
 ⅛ **teaspoon dried thyme leaves, crushed**
   Chopped fresh parsley for garnish

1. Flatten chicken to even thickness using palm of hand or flat side of meat mallet. Place 1 ham slice and 1 cheese slice on *each* breast half. Roll up chicken from narrow end, jelly-roll fashion. Tuck in ham and cheese, if necessary; secure with wooden toothpicks.

2. In 10-inch skillet over medium-high heat, in hot oil, cook chicken rolls 10 minutes or until browned on all sides. Spoon off fat.

3. Stir in soup, milk, onions and thyme. Heat to boiling. Reduce heat to low. Cover; cook 10 minutes or until chicken is no longer pink, stirring occasionally.

4. To serve, remove wooden toothpicks. Spoon some sauce over chicken rolls; pass remaining sauce. Garnish with parsley, if desired.

Makes 4 main-dish servings	Prep Time: 10 minutes Cook Time: 25 minutes

Ham-and-Cheese Turkey Rolls: Prepare Ham-and-Cheese Chicken Rolls as directed above, *except* substitute 4 *raw turkey cutlets*, about 1 pound, for the chicken. In step 2, *reduce* cooking time for browning the rolls to 5 minutes.

Ham-and-Cheese Chicken Rolls

Spanish Chicken and Rice

  2 tablespoons vegetable oil
2½- to 3-pound broiler-fryer chicken, cut up
  1 can (10½ ounces) Campbell's condensed chicken broth
  1 cup chopped green pepper
  1 can (about 8 ounces) tomatoes, drained and chopped, *or*
      ½ cup chopped fresh tomato
  ⅔ cup *uncooked* **regular long-grain rice**
  3 cloves garlic, minced
  2 tablespoons chopped pimento
  ¼ teaspoon hot pepper sauce
    Fresh parsley sprigs for garnish

1. In 10-inch skillet over medium-high heat, in hot oil, cook chicken 10 minutes or until browned on all sides. Spoon off fat.

2. Stir in broth, green pepper, tomatoes, rice, garlic, pimento and hot pepper sauce. Reduce heat to low. Cover; cook 35 minutes or until liquid is absorbed and chicken is no longer pink and juices run clear.

3. To serve, spoon some rice mixture on each plate and top with chicken. Garnish with parsley, if desired.

Makes 4 main-dish servings	Prep Time: 10 minutes Cook Time: 45 minutes

When you shop, select chicken that is plump; that's a good indication it will be moist and meaty. Also look for poultry with skin that is white to deep yellow with no bruises or discoloration.

Crispy Chicken Parmesan

4 skinless, boneless chicken breast halves *or* 8 skinless, boneless
    chicken thighs (about 1 pound)
1 egg, beaten
½ cup dry bread crumbs
2 tablespoons margarine *or* butter
1 can (10¾ ounces) Campbell's condensed broccoli cheese soup
½ cup water
1 medium tomato, sliced
1 tablespoon grated Parmesan cheese
    Sliced tomato *and* fresh fennel sprigs for garnish

1. Dip *each* chicken breast half into egg; coat with bread crumbs.

2. In 10-inch skillet over medium-high heat, in hot margarine, cook
   chicken 10 minutes on both sides or until chicken is browned and
   no longer pink. In 12- by 8-inch baking pan, arrange chicken; set
   aside.

3. In same skillet, stir soup and water. Heat through. Spoon some
   sauce over chicken. Top with tomato slices and cheese. Position
   baking pan in oven so top of chicken is 6 inches from heat. Broil 5
   minutes or until topping is hot and bubbling. Pass remaining
   sauce. Garnish with tomato and fennel, if desired.

Makes 4 main-dish servings	Prep Time: 10 minutes Cook Time: 20 minutes

Crispy Chicken Parmesan

Chicken Vegetable Sauté

2 tablespoons margarine *or* butter, divided
½ pound fresh mushrooms, thinly sliced
1 medium carrot, cut into matchstick-thin strips
4 skinless, boneless chicken breast halves (about 1 pound)
1 can (10¾ ounces) Campbell's condensed broccoli cheese soup
⅓ cup water
1 tablespoon lemon juice
⅛ teaspoon dried thyme leaves, crushed
   Fresh thyme sprigs for garnish

1. In 10-inch skillet, over medium-high heat, in *1 tablespoon* of hot margarine, cook mushrooms and carrot until tender, stirring often. Remove; keep warm.

2. In same skillet, in remaining 1 tablespoon margarine, cook chicken 10 minutes or until browned on both sides. Spoon off fat.

3. Stir in soup, water, lemon juice and thyme. Cover; cook 5 minutes or until chicken is no longer pink, stirring occasionally. Serve chicken topped with vegetables. Garnish with thyme, if desired.

Makes 4 main-dish servings	Prep Time: 15 minutes Cook Time: 20 minutes

M'm! M'm! Good!®
Beef & Pork

Foolproof Beef and Broccoli

¾ **pound boneless beef sirloin steak (about ¾ inch thick)**
1 **tablespoon vegetable oil**
1 **clove garlic, minced**
2 **cups broccoli flowerets**
1 **medium onion, cut into wedges**
1 **can (10¾ ounces) Campbell's condensed cream of broccoli soup**
¼ **cup water**
1 **tablespoon soy sauce**
   Hot cooked noodles
   Cherry tomatoes *and* fresh tarragon sprigs for garnish

1. Slice beef across grain into thin strips.

2. In 10-inch skillet over medium-high heat, in hot oil, cook beef and garlic until beef is browned. Add broccoli and onion. Cook 5 minutes, stirring often.

3. Stir in soup, water and soy sauce. Heat to boiling. Reduce heat to low. Cover; cook 5 minutes or until vegetables are tender. Serve over noodles. Garnish with cherry tomatoes and tarragon, if desired.

Makes 4 main-dish servings	Prep Time: 10 minutes Cook Time: 20 minutes

Foolproof Pork and Broccoli: Prepare Foolproof Beef and Broccoli as directed above, *except* substitute ¾ pound boneless *pork loin* for the beef. In step 2, cook 10 minutes or until vegetables are tender and pork is fork-tender.

Tip: To make slicing meat easier, freeze the beef or pork about 1 hour before cutting into thin strips.

Foolproof Beef and Broccoli

Simple Salisbury Steak

Pictured here, Simple Salisbury Steak is served with parsley-buttered noodles and steamed sliced zucchini and carrot strips. Also pictured on the back cover.

> 1 can (10¾ ounces) Campbell's condensed cream of mushroom
>   soup, divided
> 1 pound ground beef
> ⅓ cup dry bread crumbs
> ¼ cup finely chopped onion
> 1 egg, beaten
> 1 tablespoon vegetable oil
> 1½ cups sliced fresh mushrooms
>   Fresh parsley *and* halved cherry tomatoes for garnish

1. In large bowl, mix thoroughly ¼ *cup* of soup, the beef, bread crumbs, onion and egg. Shape firmly into 6 oval patties of even thickness.

2. In 10-inch skillet over medium-high heat, in hot oil, cook *half* of patties until browned on both sides. Remove; set aside. Repeat with remaining patties. Spoon off fat.

3. In same skillet, stir in remaining soup and mushrooms; return patties to skillet. Reduce heat to low. Cover; cook 20 minutes or until patties are thoroughly cooked and no longer pink, turning patties occasionally.

4. Serve patties with mushroom sauce spooned over. Garnish with parsley and cherry tomatoes, if desired.

Makes 6 main-dish servings	Prep Time: 10 minutes Cook Time: 30 minutes

Turkey Salisbury Steak: Prepare Simple Salisbury Steak as directed above, *except* substitute 1 pound ground *raw turkey* for the beef and increase *dry bread crumbs* to ½ cup.

Tip: You can substitute 1 can (about 6 ounces) sliced mushrooms and ¼ cup of mushroom liquid *or* water for the fresh mushrooms in this recipe.

Simple Salisbury Steak

Taco Salad

To personalize your Mexican-style salad, add one or more of the following: guacamole, sliced green onions, salsa, sour cream, sliced jalapeño peppers and/or sliced pitted ripe olives.

1 pound ground beef
1 pouch Campbell's dry onion quality soup and recipe mix
½ cup water
2 tablespoons chili powder
6 cups torn salad greens
    Tortilla chips
1 medium tomato, chopped
1 cup shredded Cheddar cheese (4 ounces)
    Fresh cilantro *or* parsley sprigs for garnish

1. In 10-inch skillet over medium heat, cook beef until browned and no longer pink, stirring to separate meat. Spoon off fat.

2. Stir in soup mix, water and chili powder. Heat to boiling. Reduce heat to low. Cook 10 minutes, stirring occasionally.

3. To serve, arrange lettuce on platter. Spoon hot meat mixture over lettuce. Top with chips, tomato and cheese. Garnish with cilantro, if desired.

Makes 6 main-dish servings	Prep Time: 10 minutes Cook Time: 15 minutes

Turkey Taco Salad: Prepare Taco Salad as directed above, *except* substitute 1 pound ground *raw turkey* for the beef and increase water to ⅔ *cup*. Spray skillet with *vegetable cooking spray*.

Tacos: Prepare meat mixture for Taco Salad as directed in steps 1 and 2. Spoon about ¼ *cup* of meat mixture into each of *12 warm taco shells*. Top with lettuce, tomato and cheese.

Sensational Beef Stroganoff

The choice is yours—either beef, turkey or pork can be used to make this classic Campbell recipe.

> 1 pound boneless beef top round steak (about ¾ inch thick)
> 2 tablespoons margarine *or* butter, divided
> ½ cup chopped onion
> 1 can (10¾ ounces) Campbell's condensed cream of mushroom soup
> ½ teaspoon paprika
> ½ cup sour cream *or* plain yogurt
> Hot cooked noodles
> Chopped fresh parsley, paprika, tomato wedges *and* fresh sage sprigs for garnish

1. Slice beef across the grain into thin strips.

2. In 10-inch skillet over high heat, in *1 tablespoon* of hot margarine, cook *half* of beef and *half* of onion until meat is no longer pink and onion is tender; set aside. Repeat with remaining margarine, beef and onion.

3. Return meat mixture to skillet. Stir in soup and ½ teaspoon paprika. Heat through, stirring occasionally. Remove from heat. Stir in sour cream.

4. Serve over noodles. Sprinkle with parsley and additional paprika. Garnish with tomatoes and sage, if desired.

Makes about 3½ cups or 6 main-dish servings	Prep Time: 10 minutes Cook Time: 15 minutes

Turkey Stroganoff: Prepare Sensational Beef Stroganoff as directed above, *except* substitute 1 pound *raw turkey cutlets* for the beef.

Pork Stroganoff: Prepare Sensational Beef Stroganoff as directed above, *except* substitute 1 pound boneless *pork loin* for the beef.

Tip: To make slicing meat easier, freeze the beef, turkey *or* pork about 1 hour before cutting into thin strips.

Sensational Beef Stroganoff

Savory Pot Roast

    2 tablespoons vegetable oil
3½- to 4-pound boneless beef bottom round *or* chuck pot roast
    1 can (10¾ ounces) Campbell's condensed cream of mushroom
       soup
    1 pouch Campbell's dry onion quality soup and recipe mix
1¼ cups water, divided
    6 medium potatoes, peeled and quartered
    6 carrots, cut into 2-inch pieces
    2 tablespoons all-purpose flour
    Chopped fresh parsley, matchstick-thin strips yellow squash *and*
      cherry tomatoes for garnish

1. In 6-quart Dutch oven over medium-high heat, in hot oil, cook roast until browned on all sides. Spoon off fat.

2. Stir in both soups and *1 cup* of water. Reduce heat to low. Cover; cook 2 hours or until meat is *just tender*, turning occasionally. Add potatoes and carrots. Cover; cook 40 minutes more or until roast and vegetables are tender.

3. Remove roast to platter. Arrange vegetables around roast. Cut roast across the grain. Cover and keep warm while preparing sauce.

4. Over medium heat, cook sauce until slightly thickened. In cup, stir together flour and remaining ¼ cup water until smooth. Gradually stir into sauce in Dutch oven. Cook over medium heat until mixture boils and thickens, stirring constantly.

5. Serve roast and vegetables with sauce. Sprinkle vegetables with parsley. Garnish with squash and cherry tomatoes, if desired.

Makes 8 main-dish servings	Prep Time: 5 minutes Cook Time: 3 hours

Frozen meat should be defrosted in the refrigerator, *not* at room temperature. Follow these time guidelines for defrosting meat in the refrigerator: For a large roast, allow 4 to 7 hours per pound; for a small roast, allow 3 to 5 hours per pound. To defrost meat in a microwave oven, follow manufacturer's instructions.*

*Source: Meat Board Test Kitchens & Beef Industry Council

Souper Meat Loaf

2 pounds ground beef
1 can (10¾ ounces) Campbell's condensed cream of mushroom soup, divided
1 pouch Campbell's dry onion quality soup and recipe mix
½ cup dry bread crumbs
1 egg, beaten
Broth-Simmered Vegetables (recipe follows), optional
¼ cup water
Fresh marjoram sprigs for garnish

1. In large bowl, mix thoroughly beef, *½ cup* of mushroom soup, the onion soup mix, bread crumbs and egg. In 12- by 8-inch baking pan, *firmly* shape meat mixture into 8- by 4-inch loaf.

2. Bake at 350°F. for 1¼ hours or until meat loaf is no longer pink. Meanwhile, prepare Broth-Simmered Vegetables; keep warm. Spoon off fat from meat loaf, reserving *2 tablespoons* of drippings.

3. In 1-quart saucepan over medium heat, heat remaining mushroom soup, water and reserved drippings to boiling, stirring occasionally. Thin sauce with additional water to desired consistency.

4. To serve, arrange meat loaf with vegetables on platter. Spoon some sauce over meat loaf; pass remaining sauce. Garnish with marjoram, if desired.

Makes 8 main-dish servings	**Prep Time: 5 minutes** **Cook Time: 1 hour 20 minutes**

Broth-Simmered Vegetables: In 2-quart saucepan over medium-high heat, heat ½ cup Campbell's condensed *chicken broth*, ½ cup *water* and 2 cups cut-up *fresh vegetables* or 1 package (10 to 16 ounces) *frozen vegetables* to boiling. Reduce heat to low. Cover; cook 5 minutes or until vegetables are tender. Drain. Makes 2 to 3½ cups.

Souper Meat Loaf *and*
Broth-Simmered Vegetables

London Broil with Mushroom Sauce

1½ pounds beef top round steak (about 1½ inches thick)
   2 tablespoons margarine *or* butter
   2 cups sliced fresh mushrooms
½ cup sliced onion
   1 can (10¾ ounces) Campbell's condensed cream of mushroom
      soup
¼ cup water
   2 teaspoons Worcestershire sauce
   Fluted mushrooms, celery leaves *and* orange peel for garnish

1. On unheated rack of broiler pan, place steak. Position pan in oven so top of meat is 4 inches from heat. Broil about 15 minutes for rare or until desired doneness; turn halfway through cooking.

2. Meanwhile, in 10-inch skillet over medium-high heat, in hot margarine, cook mushrooms and onion 10 minutes or until liquid evaporates and onion is browned. Stir in soup, water and Worcestershire sauce. Heat through, stirring occasionally.

3. To serve, thinly slice meat diagonally across the grain. Spoon some sauce over meat; pass remaining sauce. Garnish with mushrooms, celery leaves and orange peel, if desired.

Makes 6 main-dish servings and about 1½ cups sauce	Prep Time: 10 minutes Cook Time: 15 minutes

Follow this timetable for broiling beef steaks.*				
Cut	Approximate Thickness or Weight	Inches from Heat	Total Cooking Time in Minutes	
			140°F. (rare)	160°F. (med.)
Sirloin Steak, boneless	1 inch	3 to 4	16	21
	2 inches	4 to 5	25	30
Top Round Steak	1 inch	3 to 4	15	18
Flank Steak	1 to 1½ pounds	2 to 3	12	14

*Source: Meat Board Test Kitchens & Beef Industry Council.

London Broil with Mushroom Sauce

Herbed Pork Chops

  2 tablespoons all-purpose flour
¼ teaspoon ground sage
¼ teaspoon dried thyme leaves, crushed
  4 boneless pork chops, each cut ¾ inch thick (about 1 pound)
  2 tablespoons margarine *or* butter
  1 can (10¾ ounces) Campbell's condensed cream of chicken soup
½ cup water
    Prepared long-grain and wild rice mix *or* hot cooked rice
    Fresh thyme sprigs, orange slices, carrot curls *and* radicchio
      leaves for garnish

1. On waxed paper, combine flour, sage and thyme. Coat chops lightly with flour mixture.

2. In 10-inch skillet over medium-high heat, in hot margarine, cook chops 10 minutes or until browned on both sides. Push chops to one side of skillet. Spoon off fat.

3. Stir in soup and water, stirring to loosen browned bits. Reduce heat to low. Cover; cook 5 minutes or until chops are fork-tender.

4. Serve chops with rice; spoon sauce over. Garnish with thyme, orange slices, carrot curls and radicchio, if desired.

Makes 4 main-dish servings	Prep Time: 5 minutes Cook Time: 15 minutes

Herbed Pork Chops

Garden Pork Sauté

2 tablespoons margarine *or* butter, divided
1 pound pork tenderloin, cut into ½-inch-thick slices *or*
    4 boneless pork chops, each cut ¾ inch thick
1 cup broccoli flowerets
1 cup sliced fresh mushrooms
½ cup diagonally sliced carrot
1 can (10¾ ounces) Campbell's condensed cream of broccoli soup
⅓ cup milk
3 slices bacon, cooked and crumbled
⅛ teaspoon pepper

1. In 10-inch skillet over medium-high heat, in *1 tablespoon* of hot margarine, cook pork 10 minutes or until browned on both sides. Remove pork; keep warm.

2. In same skillet, in remaining 1 tablespoon margarine, cook broccoli, mushrooms and carrot 5 minutes, stirring often. Stir in soup, milk, bacon and pepper. Heat to boiling.

3. Return pork to skillet. Reduce heat to low. Cover; cook 5 minutes or until pork is fork-tender.

Makes 4 main-dish servings	**Prep Time: 10 minutes** **Cook Time: 20 minutes**

Onion Glorified Pork Chops

Pictured here, a single serving of Onion Glorified Pork Chops is served with parsley-buttered noodles with sautéed sliced mushrooms and cooked sugar snap peas and carrot strips.

    1 tablespoon vegetable oil
    6 pork chops, each cut ¾ inch thick (about 2 pounds)
    1 medium onion, sliced
    1 can (10¾ ounces) Campbell's condensed cream of celery soup
¼ cup water
    Sliced tomato *and* fresh parsley sprigs for garnish

1. In 10-inch skillet over medium-high heat, in hot oil, cook *half* of chops 10 minutes or until browned on both sides. Remove; set aside. Repeat with remaining chops and onion. Spoon off fat.

2. Return chops to skillet. Stir in soup and water. Reduce heat to low. Cover; cook 10 minutes or until chops are fork-tender, stirring occasionally. Garnish with tomato and parsley, if desired.

Makes 6 main-dish servings	Prep Time: 5 minutes Cook Time: 30 minutes

Mushroom Glorified Pork Chops: Prepare Onion Glorified Pork Chops as directed above, *except* substitute 1 can (10¾ ounces) Campbell's condensed *cream of mushroom soup* for the cream of celery soup. Omit onion and add 1 can (about 6 ounces) *sliced mushrooms,* drained, along with the soup.

Glazed Pork Chops

1 tablespoon margarine *or* butter
6 pork chops, each cut ¾ inch thick (about 2 pounds)
2 teaspoons cornstarch
1 cup water, divided
1 pouch Campbell's dry onion quality soup and recipe mix
2 tablespoons brown sugar
1 medium apple, cored and sliced
   Fresh marjoram sprigs for garnish

1. In 10-inch skillet over medium-high heat, in hot margarine, cook *half* of chops 10 minutes or until browned on both sides. Remove; set aside. Repeat with remaining chops. Spoon off fat.

2. Meanwhile, in cup, stir together cornstarch and ¼ *cup* of water until smooth.

3. In same skillet, combine remaining ¾ cup water, onion soup mix and sugar. Add sliced apple, stirring to coat with sauce. Heat to boiling.

4. Return chops to skillet. Reduce heat to low. Cover; cook 10 minutes or until chops are fork-tender, stirring occasionally.

5. Remove chops and apples to serving dish or platter; keep warm. Over medium heat, heat sauce mixture to boiling. Gradually stir in cornstarch mixture. Cook until mixture boils and thickens, stirring constantly. Spoon over pork and apples. Garnish with marjoram, if desired.

Makes 6 main-dish servings	Prep Time: 5 minutes Cook Time: 35 minutes

Tip: For baking and cooking, select apples that are flavorful and remain firm when heated. Choose from such varieties as Baldwin, Cortland, Granny Smith, Northern Spy, Rome Beauty and Winesap.

M'm! M'm! Good!
Side Dishes & Sauces

Pasta Primavera

   2 tablespoons margarine *or* butter
   ½ cup broccoli flowerets
   ½ cup thinly sliced carrot
   ¼ cup chopped sweet red pepper
   1 clove garlic, minced
   1 can (10¾ ounces) Campbell's condensed broccoli cheese soup
   1 cup milk
   ¼ cup grated Parmesan cheese
   3 cups hot cooked fettuccine (about 8 ounces dry)
     Sweet red pepper strips *and* fresh purple basil for garnish

1. In 10-inch skillet over medium heat, in hot margarine, cook broccoli, carrot, red pepper and garlic until vegetables are tender-crisp, stirring often.

2. Stir in soup, milk and cheese. Heat to boiling. Reduce heat to low. Cook 5 minutes, stirring occasionally. Pour soup mixture over fettuccine; toss to coat. Garnish with red pepper strips and basil, if desired.

Makes about 5 cups or 4 side-dish servings	Prep Time: 10 minutes Cook Time: 15 minutes

To microwave: In 1½-quart microwave-safe casserole, combine margarine, broccoli, carrot, pepper and garlic. Cover with lid; microwave on HIGH 4 minutes or until vegetables are tender-crisp, stirring once. Stir in soup, milk and cheese. Cover; microwave on HIGH 6 minutes, stirring once. Serve as directed in step 2.

Quick Lemon-Broccoli Rice

This fast-to-fix dish can be made with either quick-cooking white or brown rice.

  1 can (10½ ounces) Campbell's condensed chicken broth
  1 cup small broccoli flowerets
  ⅓ cup shredded carrot
1¼ cups quick-cooking rice, uncooked
  2 teaspoons lemon juice
    Generous dash pepper
    Lemon slices *and* fresh tarragon sprig for garnish

1. In 2-quart saucepan over high heat, heat broth to boiling. Add broccoli and carrot. Return to boiling. Reduce heat to low. Cover; cook 5 minutes or until vegetables are tender.

2. Stir in rice, lemon juice and pepper. Remove from heat. Cover; let stand 5 minutes or until liquid is absorbed. Fluff rice with fork before serving. Garnish with lemon slices and fresh tarragon sprig, if desired.

Makes about 3 cups or 4 servings	Prep Time: 10 minutes Cook Time: 15 minutes

Brown Rice with Broccoli: Prepare Quick Lemon-Broccoli Rice as directed above, *except* substitute *1 cup quick-cooking brown rice, uncooked,* for the quick-cooking rice. In step 1, cook rice with vegetables. In step 2, stir in 2 teaspoons chopped *fresh basil leaves or parsley* just before serving. Makes 2½ to 3 cups.

Creamy Vegetable Medley

Choose your favorite vegetable or vegetable combination to make this dish. A mixture of broccoli, asparagus, carrots and cauliflower is pictured here.

> **1 can (10¾ ounces) Campbell's condensed cream of mushroom soup**
> **1 package (16 ounces) frozen vegetable combination**

1. In 2-quart saucepan over medium heat, heat soup to boiling. Stir in vegetables.

2. Return to boiling. Reduce heat to low. Cover; cook 10 minutes or until vegetables are tender, stirring occasionally.

Makes about 3 cups or 6 side-dish servings	Prep Time: 5 minutes Cook Time: 15 minutes

To microwave: In 2-quart microwave-safe casserole, combine soup and vegetables. Cover with lid; microwave on HIGH 10 minutes or until vegetables are tender, stirring halfway through cooking. Let stand, covered, 5 minutes.

Souper Choice: Substitute 1 can (10¾ ounces) Campbell's condensed *cream of celery soup* for the cream of mushroom soup.

Creamy Mushroom Sauce

Pictured here, Creamy Mushroom Sauce is spooned over 1 pound cooked and drained fresh green beans and garnished with cherry tomatoes.

1 can (10¾ ounces) Campbell's condensed cream of mushroom soup
⅓ cup milk *or* water

In 1-quart saucepan, combine soup and milk. Over medium heat, heat until hot and bubbling, stirring often.

Makes about 1½ cups sauce or 12 servings	Prep Time: 5 minutes Cook Time: 5 minutes

Broccoli-Cheese Potato Topper

Potatoes can be baked either in the conventional oven or in the microwave oven.

1 can (11 ounces) Campbell's condensed Cheddar cheese soup
2 tablespoons sour cream *or* plain yogurt
½ teaspoon Dijon-style mustard
1 cup cooked broccoli flowerets
4 hot baked potatoes, split lengthwise
Cherry tomatoes and fresh chervil sprigs for garnish

1. In 1½-quart saucepan, combine soup, sour cream and mustard. Over medium heat, heat through, stirring occasionally. Add broccoli; heat through.

2. To serve, spoon over split potatoes. Garnish with cherry tomatoes and chervil, if desired.

Makes about 1½ cups sauce or 4 side-dish servings	Prep Time: 10 minutes Cook Time: 10 minutes

Creamy Mushroom Sauce (left) *and*
Broccoli-Cheese Potato Topper (right)

Broccoli Bake

Made with cream of broccoli soup, Broccoli Bake is a contemporary spin-off of the classic recipe, Green Bean Bake. Also pictured on the back cover.

   1 can (10¾ ounces) Campbell's condensed cream of broccoli soup
   ½ cup milk
   1 teaspoon soy sauce
      Dash pepper
   1 package (20 ounces) frozen broccoli cuts, cooked and drained
   1 can (2.8 ounces) French fried onions, divided

1. In 1½-quart casserole, combine soup, milk, soy sauce and pepper. Stir in broccoli and *½ can* of onions.

2. Bake, uncovered, at 350°F. for 25 minutes. Top with remaining onions. Bake 5 minutes more.

Makes about 4½ cups or 6 side-dish servings	Prep Time: 10 minutes Cook Time: 30 minutes

To microwave: In 1½-quart microwave-safe casserole, combine soup, milk, soy sauce and pepper. Stir in broccoli and *½ can* of onions. Cover with waxed paper; microwave on HIGH 8 minutes, rotating dish halfway through cooking. Top with remaining onions. Microwave, uncovered, on HIGH 1 minute more.

Tip: You can substitute 1 bunch (about 1½ pounds) fresh broccoli, cut up, cooked and drained *or* 2 packages (10 ounces *each*) frozen broccoli spears, cooked and drained, for the broccoli cuts.

Green Bean Bake: Prepare Broccoli Bake as directed above, *except* substitute 1 can (10¾ ounces) Campbell's condensed *cream of mushroom soup* for the cream of broccoli soup and substitute 4 cups cooked and drained *green beans* for the broccoli.

Broccoli Bake

New Potato Bake

Available spring to early summer, new potatoes are small, young potatoes of any variety. They have a crisp, waxy texture with a thin red or brown skin.

   1 can (10¾ ounces) Campbell's condensed broccoli cheese soup
  ½ cup sour cream *or* plain yogurt
  ¼ teaspoon hot pepper sauce
  7 small red potatoes (about 1½ pounds), quartered
  2 medium onions, cut into wedges
  ¼ cup grated Parmesan cheese
    Fresh chives for garnish

1. In large bowl, combine soup, sour cream and hot pepper sauce. Add potatoes and onions; toss to coat well.

2. In 2-quart oblong baking dish or 2-quart casserole, spoon potato mixture in even layer. Sprinkle with cheese. Bake at 375°F. for 50 minutes or until potatoes are fork-tender. Garnish with chives, if desired.

Makes about 6 cups or 6 side-dish servings	Prep Time: 10 minutes Cook Time: 50 minutes

To microwave: In large bowl, combine soup, sour cream and hot pepper sauce. Add potatoes and onions; toss to coat well. In 2-quart microwave-safe casserole, spoon potato mixture in even layer. Sprinkle with cheese. Cover with vented clear plastic wrap; microwave on HIGH 25 minutes or until potatoes are fork-tender, stirring halfway through cooking. Garnish as directed in step 2.

Cheddary Scalloped Potatoes

2 tablespoons margarine *or* butter
1 small onion, sliced
1 can (10¾ ounces) Campbell's condensed broccoli cheese soup
⅓ cup milk
⅛ teaspoon pepper
2 cans (about 16 ounces *each*) whole white potatoes, rinsed,
    drained and sliced
3 slices bacon, cooked and crumbled
    Chopped fresh parsley *and* parsley sprig for garnish

1. In 10-inch skillet over medium heat, in hot margarine, cook onion until tender.

2. Stir in soup, milk and pepper. Add potatoes; stir gently to coat. Heat to boiling. Reduce heat to low. Cover; cook 5 minutes or until hot and bubbling, stirring occasionally. Sprinkle with bacon. Garnish with parsley, if desired.

Makes about 3½ cups or 4 side-dish servings	Prep Time: 10 minutes Cook Time: 10 minutes

To microwave: In 1½-quart microwave-safe casserole, combine margarine and onion. Cover with lid; microwave on HIGH 2 minutes or until onion is tender. Stir in soup, milk and pepper. Add potatoes; stir. Cover; microwave on HIGH 7 minutes or until hot and bubbling, stirring halfway through cooking. Continue as directed in step 2.

Tip: You can substitute 4 medium potatoes (about 1¼ pounds), cooked and sliced (about 3½ cups), for the canned potatoes. *(Pictured)*

Cheddary Scalloped Potatoes

Cheddar Cheese Sauce

This two-ingredient sauce is versatile! Spoon it over puffy omelets, baked potatoes, French fries or cooked broccoli as pictured here.

1 can (11 ounces) Campbell's condensed Cheddar cheese soup
⅓ cup milk

In 1-quart saucepan, combine soup and milk. Over medium heat, heat until hot and bubbling, stirring often.

Makes about 1½ cups sauce or 12 servings	Prep Time: 5 minutes Cook Time: 5 minutes

Cheese Sauce Dijonnaise: Prepare Cheddar Cheese Sauce as directed above, *except* add 1 tablespoon *Dijon-style mustard* to the soup mixture.

Anytime Broccoli Cheese Sauce

Pictured here, Anytime Broccoli Cheese Sauce is poured over a cooked vegetable medley of cauliflowerets, sweet red pepper strips and sliced carrots and garnished with fresh basil.

1 can (10¾ ounces) Campbell's condensed broccoli cheese soup
⅓ cup milk

In 1-quart saucepan, combine soup and milk. Over medium heat, heat until hot and bubbling, stirring often.

Makes about 1½ cups sauce or 12 servings	Prep Time: 5 minutes Cook Time: 5 minutes

Cheddar Cheese Sauce (top) *and*
Anytime Broccoli Cheese Sauce (bottom)

STORING PERISHABLE FOODS

Follow these guidelines for storing perishable foods in the refrigerator or freezer.

- Raw meat and poultry should be wrapped securely so juices do not leak and contaminate other foods or surfaces. Since repeated handling can introduce bacteria, it's best to leave meat and poultry in the store wrapping unless the wrap is torn. Use plastic bags *over* commercial packaging.
- Date purchased food items and be sure to use them within the recommended time.
- Eggs should be stored in their carton in the refrigerator, not in the door.
- Arrange items in the refrigerator or freezer to allow air to circulate evenly.

FOOD STORAGE CHART*

These short but safe storage time limits will help keep refrigerated food from spoiling. The time limits given for frozen foods are to maintain peak flavor and texture.

Product	Refrigerator (40°F.)	Freezer (0°F.)
Eggs		
Fresh, in shell	3 weeks	Don't freeze
Raw yolks or whites	2-4 days	1 year
Hard-cooked	1 week	Don't freeze well
Soups & Stews		
Vegetable or meat-added	3-4 days	2-3 months
Meats & Poultry		
Beef roasts	3-5 days	6-12 months
Beef steaks	3-5 days	6-12 months
Lamb chops	3-5 days	6-9 months
Pork chops	3-5 days	4-6 months
Pork roasts	3-5 days	4-6 months
Stew meat–beef, lamb or pork	1-2 days	3-4 months
Ham, canned, label says "keep refrigerated"	6-9 months	Don't freeze
Ham, fully cooked, slices	3-4 days	1-2 months
Ground beef, lamb, pork, poultry or mixtures of them	1-2 days	3-4 months
Sausage, raw–beef, pork or poultry	1-2 days	1-2 months
Smoked breakfast links or patties	7 days	1-2 months
Bacon	7 days	1 month
Chicken or turkey, whole	1-2 days	1 year
Chicken or turkey, pieces	1-2 days	9 months
Cooked Meats & Poultry		
Meat or meat mixtures	3-4 days	2-3 months
Gravy or meat broth	1-2 days	2-3 months
Poultry mixtures	3-4 days	4-6 months
Poultry pieces, plain	3-4 days	4 months
Poultry pieces covered with broth/gravy	1-2 days	6 months

*Source: U.S. Department of Agriculture–Food Safety and Inspection Service.

Index

RECIPES BY SOUP